from A to B

from A to B

tales of modern motoring

photographs Martin Parr
text Nicholas Barker

BBC Books

This book is published to accompany the television series entitled FROM A TO B
which was first broadcast in March 1994

Published by BBC Books,
a division of BBC Enterprises Limited,
Woodlands, 80 Wood Lane, London W12 0TT
First published in 1994
Photographs © Martin Parr
Text © Nicholas Barker
BBC Enterprises

ISBN 0 563 36984 1

Edited and designed for BBC Books by Cornerhouse Publications, Manchester
Set in Plantin & Praxis
Printed in Great Britain by Jackson Wilson, Leeds
Colour separations by Leeds Photo Litho
Colour prints by Peter Fraser

The photographs and captions in this book are the fruits of a collaboration between the photographer Martin Parr and the BBC television series FROM A TO B – **tales of modern motoring**. Our aim was to bring together the separate media of film and photography to chronicle the thoughts, dreams and anxieties of some seventy British motorists as they plied their various journeys across different parts of the United Kingdom.

This portrait of the British road was recorded between April 1992 and October 1993. It is being presented to the public in the form of five films for BBC 2, and a nationwide photographic exhibition at Welcome Break motorway service areas.

FROM A TO B is the sequel to SIGNS OF THE TIMES – **a portrait of the nation's tastes**, a previous collaboration with Martin Parr which explored British attitudes towards 'good' and 'bad' taste in the home.

I think the Suzuki Vitara suits us because we're very outgoing. We like to go to different places and I feel that this car can get us anywhere

For most people cars play a seemingly indispensable role in their domestic and professional routines; whether to go to work or take the children to school, to drive to the supermarket or visit friends, to take off on holiday or simply travel from A to B. Cars transport us from the privacy of our homes into the public domain. They promise physical as well as social mobility, and furnish us with the most conspicuous form of personal adornment after the clothes we stand up in.

The car is second only to home ownership as the most expensive domestic acquisition. It therefore needs to be bought with care; and yet with this purchase more than most, heart and head seem destined to collide. Very rarely are car choices governed by wholly rational concerns. Matters of economy, reliability and safety compete with concerns about comfort, performance and car design. And then there are other highly subjective considerations: Is the car appropriate given one's profession and neighbourhood? Does it seem to compliment one's life-stage and general self-image?

The family are nipping over to France for the weekend. We're taking the Range Rover and we're going to drive down to the Loire to buy some wine. The Range Rover's perfect because there's room for a few cases in the back

To suggest that 'we are what we drive' is to lend weight to a cliché of 'lifestyle' journalism. Clearly we are no more reducible to the cars we drive than we are to the clothes we wear or the house we live in. However our car choices are a good deal more predictable than many of us might care to admit. We may insist that our tastes and motivations are highly 'individual' but in truth practically all of us can be caricatured and targeted by car advertisers precisely because our enthusiasms and prejudices are shared by significant numbers of like-minded people.

Let me offer myself as an example. Prior to working on this television series I never took much interest in cars. I simply used them to get from A to B. Although like most people I have a dream car (the Aston Martin DB5 featured in early James Bond films) I have never seriously considered buying a car as a personal indulgence. Hence for the last six years I have driven a bottom of the range C reg. VW Polo which has offered little comfort but has at least repaid my outlay of £3,000 by rarely breaking down.

What is significant about this choice is that for a man who professes to be both indifferent to what he drives and impervious to other people's judgments of it, the choice of a Polo was actually the 'safe' predictable purchase of a certain type of middle class professional. I did not, for example, buy a comparable Ford Fiesta or Vauxhall Nova which might have carried the stigma of a 'common' mass market British car. Nor did I select any of the highly recommended Japanese equivalents. In opting for a rival German marque instead, I was identifying with a slightly more exclusive European brand, and succumbing to a persuasive advertising campaign which promised reliability.

Equally I cannot claim to be wholly oblivious to what others think of it. To drive a car which is considerably cheaper and more dilapidated than most people on a similar salary is in itself a form of inverted snobbery. It is also a form of conspicuous restraint which is quite typical of certain people who work in the media. To be completely honest: I have the confidence to drive a diminutive VW Polo only because I live in a large house in a fashionable part of London.

It should be evident from my own reflections that car choices are informed by a complex web of loyalties and prejudices which can only be fully understood in the broader context of people's lives. The details of people's testimonies may vary greatly but their underlying concerns tend to be strikingly similar.

One of the most significant findings to have emerged from the 2000 research interviews for our last project SIGNS OF THE TIMES was the way British householders, when selecting home furnishings, tended to define their tastes in opposition to others which were actually very similar to their own. The owner of a recently purchased council house, for example, might vehemently criticise the home decorations of an existing council tenant. The 2500 research interviews conducted for FROM A TO B revealed a similar pattern. Although Volvo owners were consistently singled out as the least popular drivers, and Ladas and Reliant Robins the most risible cars, the most keenly felt criticism was generally reserved for cars which were quite similar to the complainant's. Hence

the passionate clash of opinions between owners of Sierras and Cavaliers, Mercedes and BMW, Audis and Saabs, Renault Espaces and Toyota Previas. Car loyalties are likely to be expressed with greater dogmatism than tastes in the home precisely because there is so little to distinguish one car from another.

I can flirt in my car and feel safe. This is my space so I can put my foot down and go

Driving is a quintessential modern experience, and the interior of a moving car allows for a unique form of modern story-telling. The rhythm and syntax of the driver's language is significantly affected by the demands of driving and concentrating on the road. The sense of detachment induced by car travel also encourages unusual candour and intimacy. The seventy interviews recorded on film for FROM A TO B took as their point of departure peoples' choice of cars. The agenda then broadened to embrace the totality of their experiences with cars and the journeys they made in them. Mass market models were generally selected in preference to classic and specialist cars, and as with SIGNS OF THE TIMES, care was taken to represent the scenarios and prejudices which most frequently cropped up in research.

The five films – represented in the five chapters of this book – focus on the following themes: women empowered by their car, company cars, family cars, first cars and arguing couples. A total of seventy adults and sixteen children, drawn from most parts of the United Kingdom, feature in the completed project. They were found as a result of a variety of

research techniques; chiefly advertising in magaz-
ines and newspapers, leafleting, and contacts
supplied by motoring organisations and car manufacturers. The most interesting respondents were
then filmed on camcorder as they drove on a route or
to a destination of their choice. If this was deemed
successful, transcripts of the interviews were typed
up and agreed with contributors before they were
then subjected to the more arduous ordeal of being
filmed with an entire TV crew crammed into their
car. Only once filming had been completed were
they then photographed by Martin Parr.

**When I first saw this car it belonged to the
lad living across the road. It was just the
most beautiful thing I had ever seen. I used
to look at it from my bedroom window and
think 'one day you will be mine'**

FROM A TO B does not purport to be a scientific
survey of British motorists, nor does it advance a
particular view or thesis on motoring. It simply
concedes that cars can provide both untold pleasures
and new heights of anguish and frustration. The
photographs and testimonies in this book are offered
as a mirror to the attitudes and prejudices of those
who look at them. Readers are invited to make
judgments about the people and cars on these pages.
Occasionally however they might also be confronted
by people like themselves.

NICHOLAS BARKER

LOOKING AT HIM LOOKING AT ME
women empowered by their cars

I wish someone would print a sticker that says "this is not my husband's car"

Cars are no longer a predominantly male concern. Women exercise a powerful influence on the choice of family car and company car (whether their own or their husband's). They are also, in increasing numbers, purchasing them as an indulgence. If money permits, why use the car simply to get from A to B when it can also be enjoyed as a means of display, and a source of fantasy and adventure?

To drive the car of one's choice is, for many women, a form of self-expression and a pleasurably empowering experience. Whether by retreating into a private space away from the demands of colleagues, partners or children, or by behaving in a predatory manner such as driving aggressively or soliciting the admiring glances of other motorists. The car, as many men can attest, provides unique opportunities for posing and flirting in public. Women are now using them to play similar games. From the relative safety of their vehicle they can invite the attention of strangers, secure in the knowledge that they have the power to put their foot on the accelerator pedal.

I'm no spring chicken but other drivers don't know that. All they can see is this glamorous woman behind the wheel

When discussing cars which have been purchased as an indulgence, women often liken them to a flattering article of clothing which raises their confidence and makes them feel younger. Some even point to the self-evident, though no less intriguing fact that their car only frames their head and shoulders and all but conceals the bottom half of the body. Depending on the woman's self-image, this is either a blessing or a source of disappointment.

In driving for pleasure, women do not appear to adopt different standards of driving or road etiquette to men. If anything their behaviour inclines towards the masculine stereotypes of aggression and impatience. "Women drivers" are often spoken about critically, and are commonly cited as being "unpredictable", "dangerous" and more likely to "cut them up" than men. It seems that in tasting the fruits of the motor car, women have embraced the intrinsic sensations of machine travel which have long transfixed men: power, speed and control.

If you want to drive from A to B
and feel perfectly safe with no-one looking at you, don't drive an MX5

I don't like the idea of a woman's car because that usually implies
it's small, compact, not very powerful and plenty of room for shopping.
I want something that's going to do two hundred miles down the M4, thank you

Since I've been driving I've been either going out with my husband or I've been married.
This is the first time I've driven a brand new car that I wanted,
and it suddenly dawned on me that I was no longer married

I find that other women on the road react to me in a nasty, hostile sort of way.
For some reason this hate comes across.
I mean, I give way to them so why don't they give way to me

Now that I've got the BMW I know that I fit in.
I can get into a winebar in Hampstead
a restaurant in Mayfair and a pub in Hackney

When I first bought the car I couldn't wait to catch a reflection of
myself in a shop window. It's terribly embarrassing to admit
but I really enjoyed seeing myself in the car

I think the best part of me are my legs
and obviously when I'm in the car people can't see them.
But I do like men to stare from time to time

The only difference between the Cavalier 1.6L and the Cavalier 1.6GL was a black painted strip along the back. So if I pulled up in the car park I would look like just another sales rep.

In many companies, few subjects arouse stronger passions than the company car policy. Grown men (and a not inconsiderable number of women) annually resort to puerile skirmishes in order to improve their allocation of company car.

At the heart of the problem are a few recurring grievances: do employees get enough say in their choice of car? Does their allocated car reflect their status within the company? Is it sufficiently distinguishable from those immediately below and above them in the company hierarchy? And, most urgent of all, when are they next entitled to an upgrade?

Whether a particular employee settles for a Ford Mondeo or a Vauxhall Cavalier, his main pre-occupations are likely to be with its specifications or "spec" and the corresponding "badging" on the rear of the car. Here is proof of his position in the company, and reassurance about how highly his employers regard him.

The world of the company car has spawned an unusual form of connoisseurship in which arcane details such as metallic paint, alloy wheels, electric windows, sun roofs, fog lamps and rear head restraints become crucial markers of the company pecking order. Although such minutiae mean little to the uninitiated, the seasoned company car man can judge another man's car "spec" from fifty yards on a motorway.

The clearest indication of the size of a car's engine and its level of specification is the chrome badge on the back. However appearances can be deceptive. Many company car drivers (particularly of Mercedes and BMW) remove these badges. The aim is either to feign greater engine size than they actually possess or, in the case of some senior managers, to conceal from clients and colleagues the fact that they are driving a top of a range model.

Nor is this deception restricted to the more 'exclusive' company car marques. Many drivers of bottom of the range mass model admit to changing their car's badging by sticking additional chrome insignia onto the backs of their cars.

Such antics cannot simply be dismissed as a neurotic preoccupation with status. The businessman or sales rep knows to his cost that prospective clients are likely to judge his seniority and professional competence on the basis of the car that he pulls up in. The owners of lowly company cars regularly confess to parking them out of sight of clients in order to safeguard the day's business. It is perhaps no surprise that so many of these men spend countless hours on the motorway lost in a reverie as they plot to out manoeuvre their company car manager.

I drive an Astra CDi and I'm a National Business Development Manager
for a company that manufactures jams, marmalades, gourmet accompaniments and food gifts

When I'm on the motorway I don't day-dream.
I'm usually thinking of the fuel range I've got on board
and where my next Little Chef stop will be.
They really do have all the things a rep needs

One of the first points a rep looks for in a car is a hook to hang his jacket up on.
I reckon that if a car didn't have that feature, a rep wouldn't even look at it

Obviously my wife knew that I was getting a new company car.
When I told her it was a Maestro Diesel Clubman,
we both literally sat down and cried – we physically cried.
Going from the Vauxhall Cavalier down to this,
I just wondered what I'd done to deserve it

I tend to daydream and drift away and imagine I'm driving something a little better.
You have to drift away in this car otherwise you'd go mad

Some of the journeys – Jesus Christ, the monotonous ones – you tend to switch off.
I can go through a city like Sheffield or Leeds and you suddenly think
"Have I been through Leeds yet? Have I been through bloody Sheffield?
Which way did I come?"

I like to think I'm quite successful because I've got a Cavalier 2 litre GLi.
I sell industrial packaging machines – something with a bit of esteem
not like Derek in Coronation Street who sells novelty items out of a bloody suitcase

I think people generally assume that if you're in a Sierra or a Cavalier
you're a rep racing to get home early for his tea.
Whereas if you're driving a BMW you're an important executive
on his way to another important meeting

I managed to persuade my boss to give me the BMW by a sort of
long-term drip feed effect. I commented on his own nice leather upholstery
and said that if he really wanted to motivate his new employee,
shouldn't this be something that he should be considering?
And it worked

Yes, it's an estate car and estate cars are boring. But I think the Audi is the sexiest available. I think it looks quite sporty and I enjoy driving it

With the arrival of children, a couple must reevaluate the suitability of their car and contemplate a significant shift in their self-image as a family. Dreams of squeezing a babyseat into the back of a two-seater sports car quickly disappear once the volume of baby paraphernalia has been fully grasped. With the second or third child, the complete transformation of car travel from a relatively sedate experience into a chaotic assault course, forces parents to contemplate car purchases which might previously have been unthinkable.

The poor image of the family car as a boring, practical "box on wheels" has been addressed by car manufacturers with invention and vigour in recent years. Estate cars have become sportier. Four-wheel drives have forsaken their work-horse origins and have been marketed as playful family cars, and vans have metamorphosed into futuristic 'people carriers'.

When I see a family in a Vitara I always imagine they're going somewhere fun and not just going to the supermarket like you would if they were in a Volvo or a Fiesta

The traditional method of selling family cars was to convince the male 'head of household' that beneath the practical exterior of the family saloon or estate lay a younger, virile, more exciting car. The advertising slogan "Satisfy your other half" was perhaps the apotheosis of this strategy.

Over the past five years however there has been a significant shift in the representation of family motoring. The promise of fun and holiday adventure – previously the mainstay of advertising to young car buyers – has been directed at the family car market. Parents of 2.4 children can now seemingly have it all. The modern family car, in addition to being safe and reliable, will enable them to "get-up-and-go", and at a moment's notice embrace all manner of exciting new pastimes.

I'd like my dad to have a change from Volvo because since I was a baby, all I can remember is having a Volvo

Although parents may be delighted with the new model on the drive, junior members of the family may be less than happy. Children as young as five or six now volunteer suggestions about a better or more appropriate family car (my own six year old has set her heart on 'three rows of seats'). As they get older so the phenomenon of 'pester-power' increases. Indeed so ashamed are some teenagers of the family Skoda or plush Mercedes that they even insist on being dropped off some distance from the school gates to avoid being seen by their friends.

I suppose we've always got this dream about selling the house and just taking off.
In an ordinary car we'd probably get as far as the ferry and come back.
But with a Land Rover we could pack everybody in it and just go

The sooner we get rid of the Mercedes the better.
It's too smooth. I think we're more of a rough and ready family.
We don't suit this car at all

When I say "When are we there Dad",
he says "Oh, we'll be there in about five minutes"
and then it takes us about an hour

Before the recession we had a Montego Estate which we were madly in love with.
That was the hardest part, going from a decent car to this.
It's like wearing a placard round your neck saying we're poor

All my friends' parents have got normal cars, like Escorts and stuff.
But these are the worst because they just stick out so much. It's really embarrassing

My Dad's got a Volvo. My Uncle's got a Volvo. My Grandad's got a Volvo.
I can't think of anyone else but I'm sure if my Nana could drive she'd probably have a Volvo

A lot of people don't like Volvos.
A lot of people wouldn't dream of going out and buying one.
But it suits us as a family and as far as I'm concerned we're sticking with Volvo

Buying the Espace represents the most daring thing we've ever done.
Although we like to think we're "get-up-and-go" people who go everywhere,
we never really do anything that's very adventurous

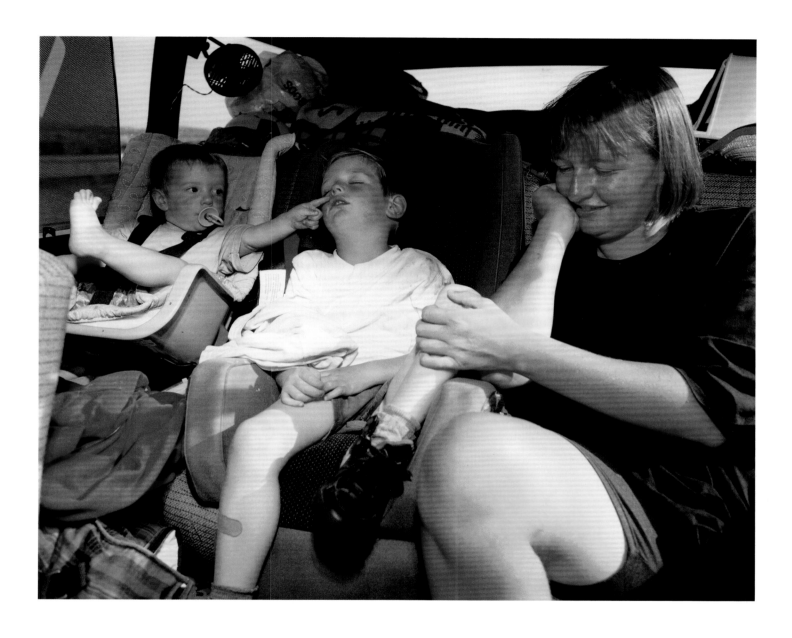

When we went to test drive the Renault Espace, Betty needed a feed so I got into the back.
It was just the ultimate breast feeding car. There was so much space

IT GETS YOU OUT THE HOUSE
first cars

I was previously restricted – sort of chained up in the house. Now I can go out whenever I want

Passing one's driving test is a significant rite of passage for young people. Sixteen may be the age of consent and eighteen the year of the franchise but at seventeen, the opportunity to gain a driver's licence provides most teenagers with dramatic and tangible proof of their adulthood.

Although the first car is evidence of maturity, it is also paradoxically a new means for expressing one's youth. It literally transports its young driver out of the home, and provides a new source of privacy to rival the childhood bedroom. Music can now be played at volume, sexuality explored without disturbance, and all manner of bad habits indulged.

I was driving down this dual carriageway doing my hair and putting on my spot cream when I ran straight under the back of a lorry

Many young drivers have an accident within weeks of starting to drive. For those with only third party insurance, the promise of independence and new freedom is quickly replaced by unexpected debt, loss of mobility and – worst of all – increased dependence on parents. In many households, the prospect of a teenager starting to drive raises awareness of changing family roles and the imminent end to childhood. Decisions about a suitable car to buy commonly unlock a Pandora's box of conflicting expectations.

Parents generally want something practical and 'safe' which will not be a drain on their own or their child's resources. Financial assistance is often offered but almost always with strings attached: some say is generally demanded over what vehicle is bought, and a common form of blackmail links the car to successful exam results or a pledge to continue their education.

Even if a teenager is happy with these terms, further family squabbles may ensue. There may be an outbreak of sibling rivalry ("how come I get a boring Fiesta when my brother got a B reg. XR2"?) or the parents themselves may fail to agree on the choice of an appropriate first car. At the very moment when teenagers are first experimenting with adulthood, parents may be looking back with nostalgia on their own teen years. It is not without significance that many fathers encourage their sons to buy the car which they themselves drove when they began dating their future wives.

Teenagers are generally single-minded about their choice of first car. They recognise that their options are limited by financial constraints (insurance premiums are often higher than the value of the car itself), but they are acutely aware of the cars driven by their peers. Their car needs to fit in with the gang, and ideally strike an impressive pose. To this end hundreds of hours may be spent on painstaking DIY improvements. Any suggestion that they might drive a car which they consider too posh, too scruffy, too "naff", or too middle-aged, is likely to be greeted with scorn and disbelief.

Buying the Beetle is the first really big mistake I've made.
Now I won't buy anything without checking it over.
A bit like my Dad in that way. But don't tell him that

The Burger King car park is where everyone hangs out.
I'm young, I'm single, I'm having fun before it's too late.
I've got the rest of my life to be old

As far as my social life is concerned the Metro is a no-go area.
I think I'd look so much better sat in an XR2

For his 21st birthday my husband offered James an upgrade on his Renault Clio.
James thought "upgrade" meant something "snazzier"
and my husband thought "something safer with more metal around you".
When they discovered what the other was thinking there was two months of total warfare

I can't show off to my friends because, without trying to sound obnoxious,
they're sort of staggeringly rich and have absurd cars.
So I did want to keep my end up slightly
and I thought the Clio 16v was good enough to get by on

My parents want to keep me wrapped up in cotton wool and they want to protect me.
Buying me this car is their way of doing it

After the car the next thing my parents bought for me was a portable phone
which they insisted I had in the car in case of emergency.
And also to tell them if I was going to be late home

Mum was really gutted.
She said she never thought I'd drop so low as to become a car thief

These days when I'm driving along,
my music's on, my mind's blank, I'm well happy, – no worries.
When I was nicking cars I had to look over my shoulder every few minutes

SHE LIKES IT HOT
arguing couples

Many couples admit to experiencing their worst arguments during car journeys. Whether the car or the relationship is responsible, what seems indisputable is the way cars heighten the moods and sensibilities of the people they carry. A journey may start out as a relaxing or exhilarating experience and then unexpectedly develop into a highly stressful ordeal. The promise of the open road may with equal unpredictability disintegrate into a traffic jam from which there is no possibility of escape.

I think we could spend the money better on having a family car or building my kitchen extension. Look how long I've had to wait for my extension because you wanted this Turbo car

The antiquated notion that men should automatically select, pay for and then act as chief custodian of the family car has been challenged by changing social values and the growing incidence of dual income, two-car families. However the car remains a common launchpad for domestic power struggles. Although women are encouraged by advertisers to be independent and assertive car buyers, once married they quickly discover that car salesmen prefer to address their husbands. A woman's problems may then be compounded either because her husband claims a superior knowledge of cars to her own, or because his zealous interest in a particular model conflicts with more pressing family needs. A common complaint concerns the reluctance of husbands to exchange cherished hatchbacks or coupés for a more appropriate family car.

She leaves them in the bedroom, in her coat pocket, in the toilet, in the shopping. She's left them down the side of the settee, in her shoes. And we've even found them in the fridge

Even before the first word is spoken in the car, many couples find that one of two issues has already guaranteed an argumentative start to the journey. Who mislaid the car keys? And which of them is most responsible for their always being late? Once these questions have been resolved, there remains ample potential for further car-related disagreement: standards of driving and car cleanliness, road directions, map reading, heat and air control, seat and mirror adjustments, choice of music, and leaving the car with the petrol gauge hovering above empty.

Cars were not designed for normal conversation. Seats are close yet separate, eye contact is minimal, and the shared view through a glass windscreen is alternately unreal and frighteningly possible – rather like television. In this confined setting heated words often give way to an angry silence.

Ken's slow. I think its his age.
When we're driving on the motorway everything belts past us
and he's chugging along at fifty-five on the inside lane

The wife, she thinks I mess over it too much.
I wash it every Sunday. It's a religion with me.
You never know, it could be worth a lot of money one day

She's one of these ladies, she's very strong-willed you know.
She thinks things should be done her way,
but when she's driving this car they've got to be done my way.
That's top and tail of it

I drive a rather excellent BMW 735i.
It's a dark black, fully-loaded, executive autobahn express.
My wife drives a rather diminutive Fiat Panda which is best not described

Every time I drove the car you were always in a mood
but then I realised that it was your male ego.
So I let you drive now

When it comes to cars Denyse will always choose something posh,
something to show she's got money, that she's making it up the old social ladder so to speak,
whereas I prefer a bit of an old banger

Because she's a driving instructor, she's a bloody nightmare to drive with.
She's always picking faults, and worse still she's got a dual transmission
and she actually uses the brake to stop the car

I often look at his car and think
"My God he doesn't have to grow up and I do".
He can just take off on his own and I have to jump into the family car with all the children

Special thanks to

Lucy Blakstad, Amanda Prince, Ben Gale, Sophie Manham, Gabrielle Osrin and
Jackie Humphries who collectively developed the television series
FROM A TO B and found the people featured in the films and this book

Joanne Stubbs who coordinated both projects

Alan Yentob who commissioned the films and Paul Hamann who provided
loyal assistance

Nigel Horne and Michael Collins of the Daily Telegraph Magazine who
supported Martin Parr's still photography for FROM A TO B

Welcome Break who sponsored the accompanying exhibition
at their motorway service areas

Dewi Lewis at Cornerhouse Publications who advised on all aspects of the book

And finally the many motorists who generously gave us access to their
thoughts and their cars whilst patiently enduring the technical and
logistical difficulties of making FROM A TO B